Contents

Nursery rhymes

Hey, diddle dumpling 2
Wee Willie Winkie 3
Elsie Marley 4
Hickory dickory dock 4
Twinkle, twinkle, little star 5
Sing a song of sixpence 6
Six little mice 8

Action rhymes

Two fat gentlemen met in a lane 9
One, two, three, four, five 10
The church 11
Five little soldiers 12
Here are the lady's knives and forks 13
Incey Wincey Spider 14
Teddy bear, teddy bear 15
I'm a little teapot 16

 finger rhymes

Hey, diddle dumpling

Diddle, diddle, dumpling,
  my son John,
Went to bed with his trousers on,
One shoe off and one shoe on,
Diddle, diddle, dumpling,
  my son John.

Wee Willie Winkie

Wee Willie Winkie runs
 through the town,
Upstairs and downstairs
 in his night-gown,
Rapping at the window,
 crying through the lock,
Are the children all in bed,
 for it's now eight o'clock?

Elsie Marley

Elsie Marley is grown so fine,
She won't get up to feed the swine,
But lies in bed till eight or nine.
　　Lazy Elsie Marley.

Hickory dickory dock

Hickory dickory dock,
The mouse ran up the clock.
The clock struck one,
The mouse ran down.
Hickory dickory dock.

Twinkle, twinkle, little star

Twinkle, twinkle, little star,
How I wonder what you are!
Up above the world so high,
Like a diamond in the sky.

Sing a song of sixpence

Sing a song of sixpence,
A pocket full of rye,
Four-and-twenty blackbirds,
Baked in a pie.

When the pie was opened,
The birds began to sing.
Was that not a dainty dish,
To set before a king?

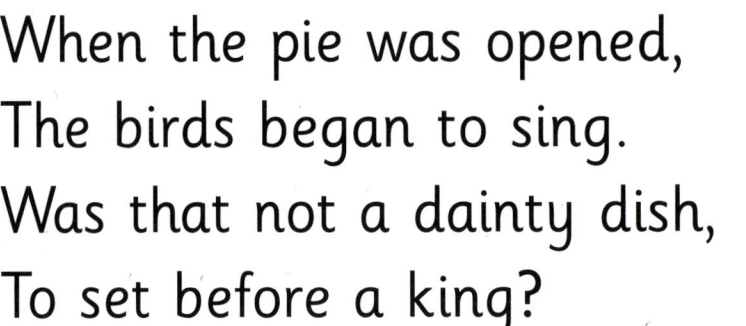

The King was in his counting house
Counting out his money,
The Queen was in the parlour
Eating bread and honey.

The maid was in the garden,
Hanging out the clothes,
When down came a blackbird
And pecked off her nose.

Six little mice

Six little mice sat down to spin,
Pussy passed by and she peeped in.
What are you doing, my little men?
Weaving coats for gentlemen.
Shall I come in and cut off your threads?
No, no, Mistress Pussy, you'd bite off
   our heads.
Oh no, I'll not. I'll help you to spin.
That may be so, but you don't come in.

Two fat gentlemen met in a lane

Two fat gentlemen met in a lane,
Bowed most politely, bowed once again.
How do you do? How do you do?
How do you do again?

Two thin ladies met in a lane …

Two tall policemen met in a lane …

Two little schoolboys met in a lane …

Two little babies met in a lane …

 # One, two, three, four, five

One, two, three, four, five,
Once I caught a fish alive.
Six, seven, eight, nine, ten,
Then I let it go again.
Why did you let it go?
Because it bit my finger so.
Which finger did it bite?
This little finger on my right.

The church

Here is the church,
And here's the steeple,
Open the doors,
And see all the people.

Here is the parson
Going upstairs,
And here is the parson
Saying his prayers.

Incey Wincey Spider

Incey Wincey Spider
Climbed up the spout,
Down came the rain
And washed the spider out,
Out came the sunshine
And dried up all the rain,
Incey Wincey Spider
Climbed up the spout again.

Teddy bear, teddy bear

Teddy bear, teddy bear, touch your nose,
Teddy bear, teddy bear, touch your toes,
Teddy bear, teddy bear, touch the ground,
Teddy bear, teddy bear, turn around.

Teddy bear, teddy bear, climb the stairs,
Teddy bear, teddy bear, say your prayers,
Teddy bear, teddy bear, turn off the light,
Teddy bear, teddy bear, say goodnight!

I'm a little teapot

I'm a little teapot,
Short and stout,
Here's my handle,
Here's my spout.
When I get steam up,
Hear me shout,
Tip me up
And pour me out.